NATHANIEL BRANDEN'S

Little Blue Book of

# SELF-ESTEEM

Nathaniel Branden's

# Little Blue Book of SELF-ESTEEM

Barnes & Noble Books
New York

This edition published by Barnes & Noble, Inc.
by arrangement with Nightingale-Conant Corp.

1995 Barnes & Noble Books

ISBN 1-56619-863-1

Book design by Rocket Design, James Sarfati

Printed and bound in the United States of America

2 4 6 8 10 M 9 7 5 3 1

# About the Author

Nathaniel Branden has been described as "the father of self-esteem." Over thirty years ago he began his pioneering work that led to the discovery of self-esteem's impact on human well-being. Born in Toronto, Canada and educated in the United States, Dr. Branden received his Ph.D. in psychology in 1973 at the California Graduate Institute. His first major work, *The Psychology of Self-Esteem*, was published in 1969 and is now a classic of the genre and in its thirtieth printing. Since then, Dr. Branden's innovative approach to raising self-esteem has seen its way to print many times, resulting in the bestselling *Honoring the Self*, *The Psychology of Romantic Love*, and *The Power of Self-Esteem*. His pioneering technique of stimulating the individual's capacity for self-healing has been adopted the world over by psychologists, psychotherapists, and motivational experts.

# Nathaniel Branden Quotations

Self-esteem pertains to how you experience yourself, not how other people think or feel about you.

Genuine self-esteem is you trusting you, you believing in you, and you having confidence in your own mind and your own ability to judge.

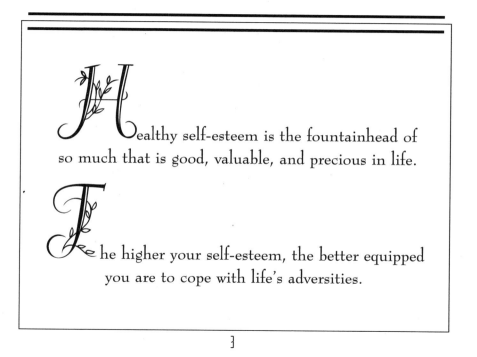

Healthy self-esteem is the fountainhead of so much that is good, valuable, and precious in life.

The higher your self-esteem, the better equipped you are to cope with life's adversities.

Self-esteem has to do with real battles won, real issues confronted, real courage, real honesty, real integrity. It is not simply getting some kind of a quick fix.

Self-esteem has tremendous power to enrich our lives, to make us more effective, to make us more open to love, to make us rise to the stars in our work, to really achieve great things.

The fact that we are alive is the basic source of our right to strive for happiness.

For good or for ill, self-concept is destiny.

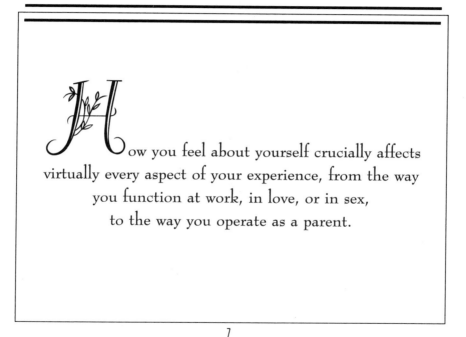

How you feel about yourself crucially affects virtually every aspect of your experience, from the way you function at work, in love, or in sex, to the way you operate as a parent.

High self-esteem people are primarily oriented toward challenge and opportunity.

You have to leave the place where you began to become more fully who you can be.

Your responses are shaped by who and what you think you are. Self-esteem is the key to success or failure, and it is also the key to understanding yourself and other people.

Of all the judgments you pass, none is as important as the one you pass on yourself. Positive self-esteem is a major requirement for a fulfilling life.

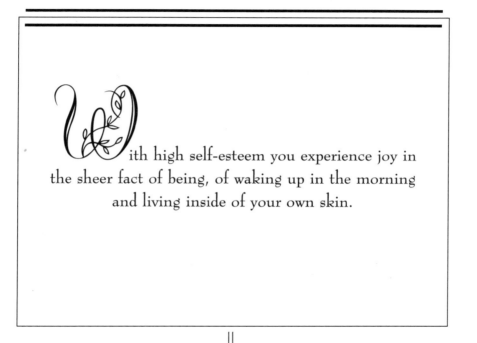

With high self-esteem you experience joy in the sheer fact of being, of waking up in the morning and living inside of your own skin.

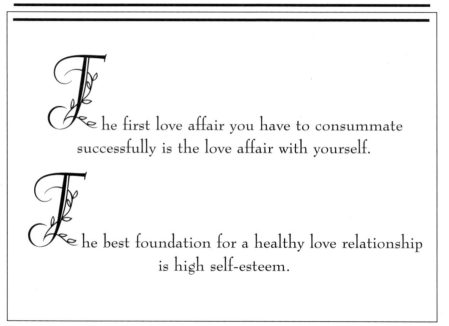

The first love affair you have to consummate successfully is the love affair with yourself.

The best foundation for a healthy love relationship is high self-esteem.

If you don't love yourself, it is exceedingly difficult to really love another person. And if you don't love yourself, it is very difficult to fully believe or accept that another person loves you.

The higher your self-esteem, the more likely it is that you will be innovative rather than ritualistic and tradition-bound in your work. This ensures greater success in a world of increasingly rapid change.

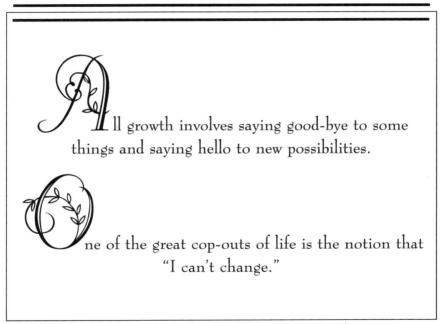

All growth involves saying good-bye to some things and saying hello to new possibilities.

One of the great cop-outs of life is the notion that "I can't change."

We all operate out of a self-fulfilling prophecy. How we see ourselves determines what our expectations are. What our expectations are determines how we are likely to act. How we act determines the kind of results we are likely to have.

If you don't like your life now, write a list of what you don't like about it and begin to develop some strategies for getting out of it.

The words "live consciously" best describe what we can do to raise our self-esteem and generate more self-confidence and self-respect.

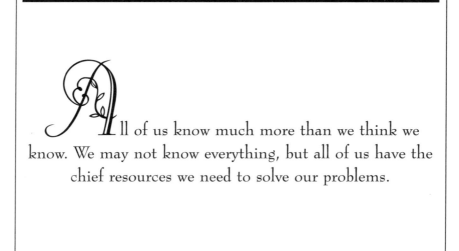

All of us know much more than we think we know. We may not know everything, but all of us have the chief resources we need to solve our problems.

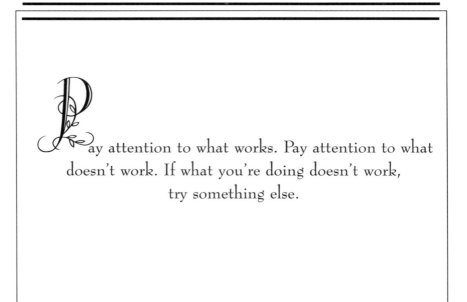

Pay attention to what works. Pay attention to what doesn't work. If what you're doing doesn't work, try something else.

Self-esteem is a function, not of what we are born with, but of how we use our consciousness—the choices we make concerning awareness, the honesty of our relationships to reality, the level of our personal integrity.

You can't live just mimicking what your mother or father value. Even if in the end you come to agree with them, you still have to make a fresh discovery for yourself if you are to achieve full human stature.

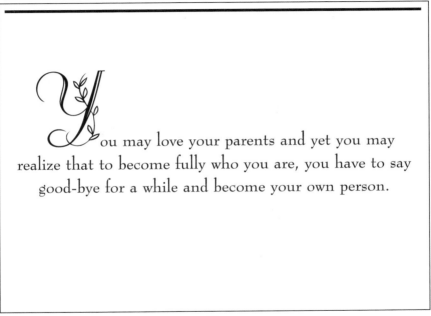

You may love your parents and yet you may realize that to become fully who you are, you have to say good-bye for a while and become your own person.

In being authentic, we not only honor ourselves—we offer a gift to whomever we deal with.

Living consciously implies respect for the facts of reality—the facts of our inner world as well as the outer world.

We can learn to recognize and make friends with the child within ourselves by listening attentively to what the child needs to tell us, even if it is painful.

You can hardly feel good about yourself if you are wandering around in a self-induced mental fog. If you attempt to exist unthinkingly, your sense of worthiness suffers, regardless of anyone else's approval or disapproval.

The mind is our basic means of survival. All our distinctively human accomplishments are the reflection of our ability to think.

The appropriate use of our consciousness is not automatic. It is an act of choice. We can choose to see more or less; we can wish to know or not to know.

Full, sincere acceptance tends to act, in time, as a dissolvent of negative or unwanted feelings such as pain, anger, envy, or fear.

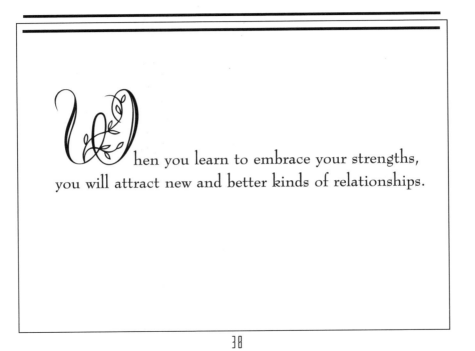

When you learn to embrace your strengths, you will attract new and better kinds of relationships.

If you love somebody, you have to respect his or her individuality and uniqueness. Understand that he or she is not a mirror image of you and will not always behave exactly as you would behave.

Be keenly conscious of the precedents that are being set in any relationship. It is far easier to change a precedent that has not yet been fully fixed than one that has been operative for thirty years.

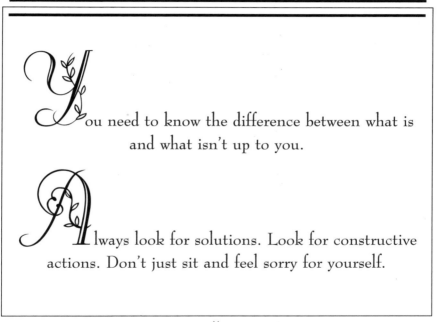

You need to know the difference between what is and what isn't up to you.

Always look for solutions. Look for constructive actions. Don't just sit and feel sorry for yourself.

If you want to learn to think independently, you have to learn to be more honest about what you really feel. If you want to learn to trust your own mind, you need to be truthful with yourself about what you really want.

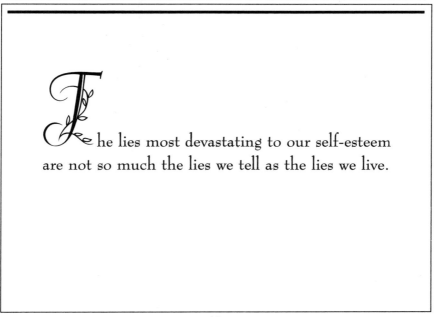

The lies most devastating to our self-esteem are not so much the lies we tell as the lies we live.

You have to be sensitive to what is happening inside of yourself. You have to be willing to know how you feel about things, how things affect you, what brings you joy, and what brings you pain.

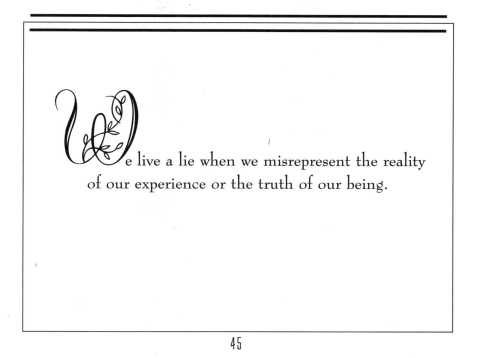

We live a lie when we misrepresent the reality of our experience or the truth of our being.

Honor your own wants; honor your own life. Always be alert to your inner signals. Don't act impulsively, but pay attention. Sometimes one part of your mind is years ahead of another part in its wisdom.

Follow that which evokes ecstasy in you. Follow that which brings out the best in you, that which energizes and charges you and will direct you to the best path for you.

You have the ability to surrender to your feelings, and you have the ability to transcend them.

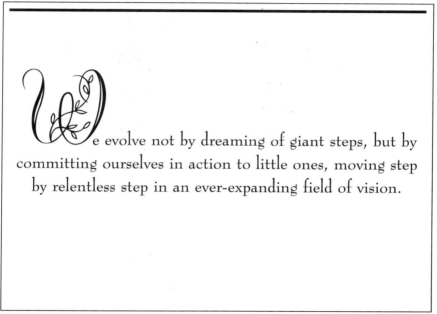

We evolve not by dreaming of giant steps, but by committing ourselves in action to little ones, moving step by relentless step in an ever-expanding field of vision.

The more active we are, rather than passive, the more we like ourselves, trust ourselves, feel competent to live and deserving of happiness.

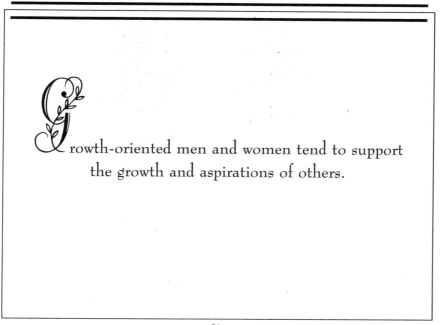

Growth-oriented men and women tend to support the growth and aspirations of others.

If you want to nurture the self-esteem of another person, you need to relate to that person from your own idea of his or her worth and value, and provide an experience of acceptance and respect.

Men and women who enjoy high self-esteem have an active orientation toward life rather than a passive one. They take full responsibility for the attainment of their desires. They don't wait for others to fulfill their dreams.

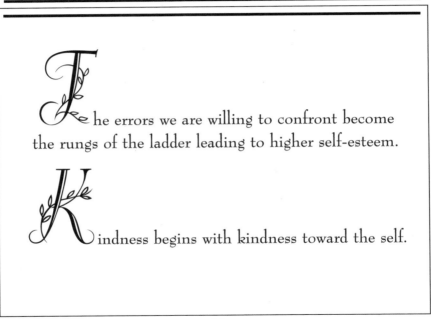

The errors we are willing to confront become the rungs of the ladder leading to higher self-esteem.

Kindness begins with kindness toward the self.

You have a right to your feelings. Your feelings are there to tell you something, but they are not infallible guides to behavior.

Accepting doesn't mean liking or approving. It means letting in the full reality—this is the way it is right now, this is where I am, this is what I did, this is what I think, this is what I feel.

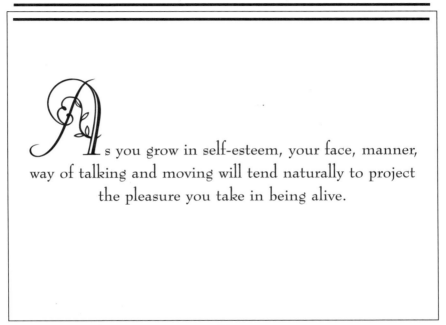

As you grow in self-esteem, your face, manner, way of talking and moving will tend naturally to project the pleasure you take in being alive.

Relaxation comes when you are not hiding from yourself and aren't at war with who you are.

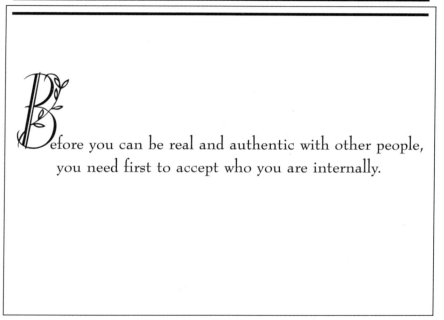

Before you can be real and authentic with other people, you need first to accept who you are internally.

The way you think about your behavior, the standards by which you judge it, and the context in which you see it are vitally important—especially at times when you are likely to condemn yourself.

Life, growth, and change all go together. Enhance it. Welcome it. It is all part of the great, fabulous adventure of life. Don't put yourself down for your fears. Respect your fears.

Suffering is just about the easiest of all human activities; being happy is just about the hardest. And happiness requires, not surrender to guilt, but emancipation from guilt.

Serenity inspires serenity, happiness inspires happiness, openness inspires openness. And when we live from the best within ourselves, we are most likely to draw out the best in others.

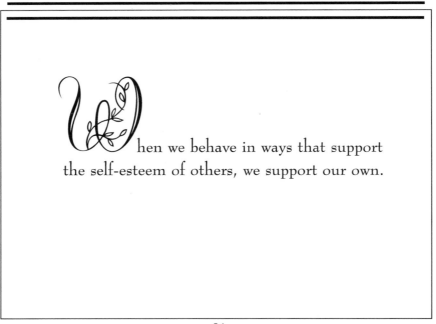

When we behave in ways that support the self-esteem of others, we support our own.

One of the best things you can do to support the self-esteem of another person is to really let that person know that when he or she is speaking, you are listening.

The real challenge is to sense people's strengths that they themselves may not know about.

Individualism isn't the adversary of community, but its most vital pillar.

You can accept a person's feelings without sharing them. You can accept the fact that this is what a person thinks without agreeing.

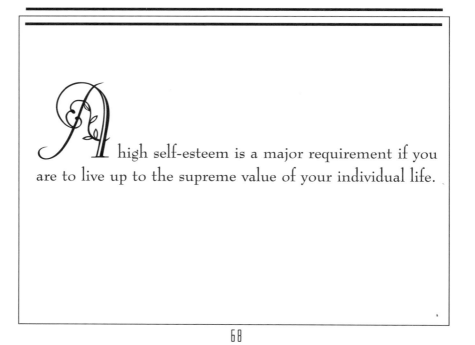

A high self-esteem is a major requirement if you are to live up to the supreme value of your individual life.

Self-esteem isn't determined by worldly success, physical appearance, popularity, or anything we can't entirely choose for ourselves. But it is a function of our honesty, integrity, and rationality—and these we have control over.

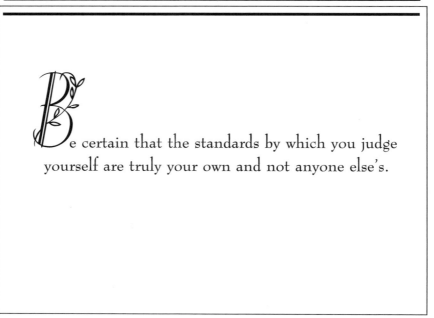

Be certain that the standards by which you judge yourself are truly your own and not anyone else's.

Positive self-esteem is the feeling, experience, and conviction we have of being appropriate to life and to the challenges of life.

Self-acceptance is the foundation of all growth and change. It is the courage, in the ultimate sense, to be for ourselves. The level of our self-esteem cannot be higher than the level of our self-acceptance.

Some things you have control over; others you don't. If you hold yourself responsible for matters beyond your control, your self-esteem will suffer. If you deny responsibility for matters that are within your control, you will jeopardize your self-esteem.

Integrity is the integration of convictions, standards, beliefs, and behavior. When your behavior expresses your professed values, you have integrity.

It takes courage to work at liberating yourself from guilt. It takes honesty and independence—and living consciously, authentically, responsibly, and actively—but it can be done.

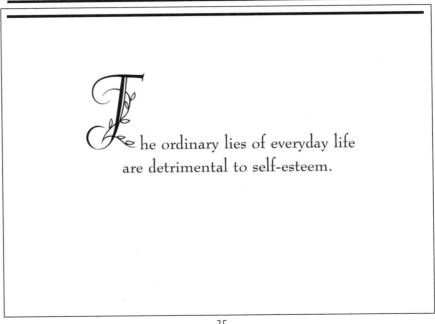

The ordinary lies of everyday life are detrimental to self-esteem.

The central pillar of healthy self-esteem is a policy of living consciously. This entails rationality, honesty, and integrity. Living consciously is living responsibly toward reality—living with a respect for facts, knowledge, and truth.

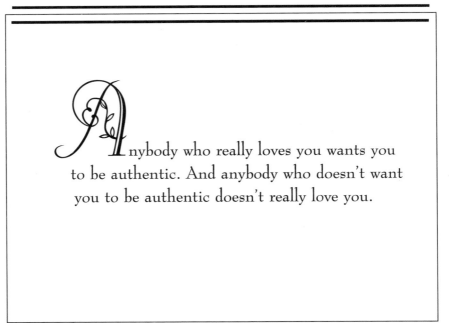

Anybody who really loves you wants you to be authentic. And anybody who doesn't want you to be authentic doesn't really love you.

Live self-assertively. Bring into the world that which you think, value, and feel. Do not consign yourself to the underground of the unexpressed and unlived.

If you have a high level of self-respect, it is very natural and comfortable for you to treat others with respect.

The essence or core of inner strength is self-esteem—belief in yourself, confidence in your own thinking, belief in your ability to learn and master whatever life requires you to learn and master.

The real motor behind achievement is confidence in yourself and confidence in your efficacy.

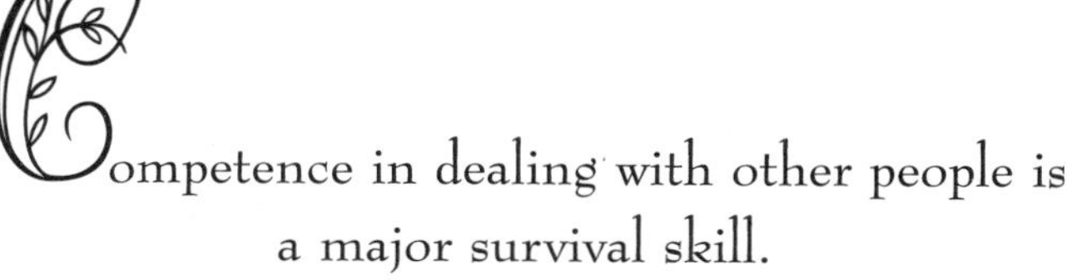

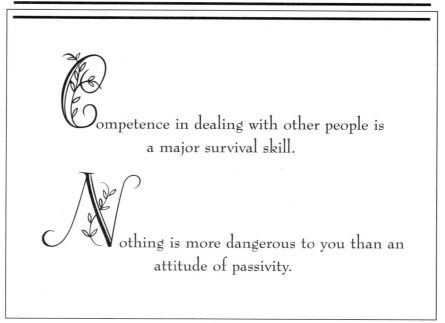

Competence in dealing with other people is a major survival skill.

Nothing is more dangerous to you than an attitude of passivity.

The real, basic power of an individual isn't what he or she knows, it is the ability to think and the ability to learn and the ability to face new challenges.

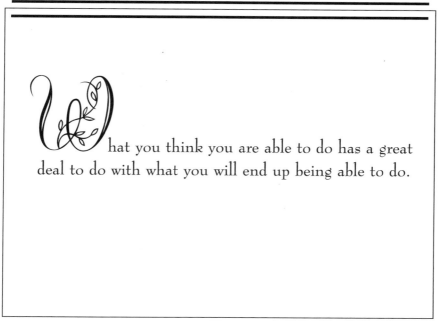

What you think you are able to do has a great deal to do with what you will end up being able to do.

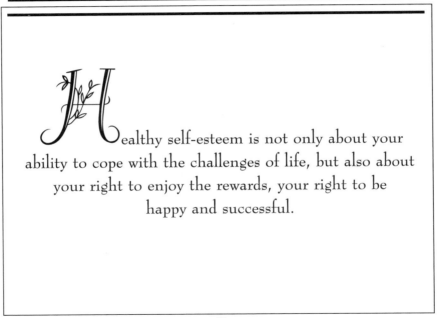

Healthy self-esteem is not only about your ability to cope with the challenges of life, but also about your right to enjoy the rewards, your right to be happy and successful.

Self-acceptance doesn't mean I like or admire everything about myself; it is an overall attitude of being for myself, of being on my own side.

If you feel lovable and worthy of happiness, you have an emotional benevolence that you bring to relationships.

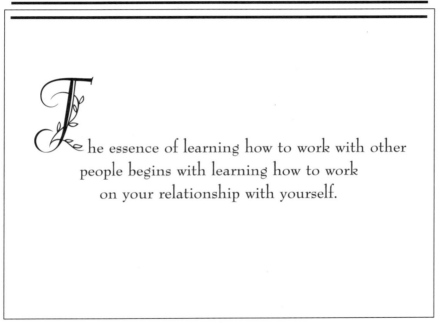

The essence of learning how to work with other people begins with learning how to work on your relationship with yourself.

Poor self-esteem doesn't necessarily prevent you from being a high achiever, but it will prevent you from enjoying your achievements.

Self-esteem is trust in your own mind. Self-esteem is the conviction of your right to be happy.

Acceptance is not the enemy of change, it is the precondition of change.

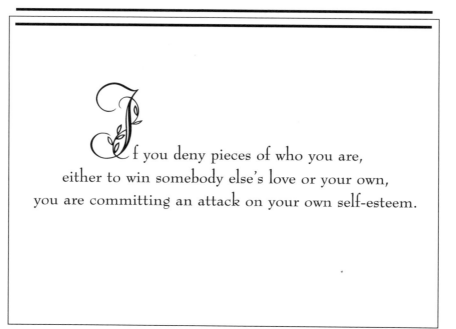

If you deny pieces of who you are,
either to win somebody else's love or your own,
you are committing an attack on your own self-esteem.

People who are ambitious are always looking at the wider picture. They look for opportunities to contribute. They look for what needs to be done.

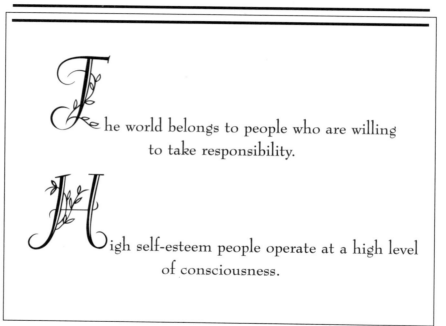

The world belongs to people who are willing to take responsibility.

High self-esteem people operate at a high level of consciousness.

You are not likely to bring out the best in people and to nurture their creativity and self-esteem if every time you hear about their problems you instantly give a solution. Encourage people to look for their own solutions.

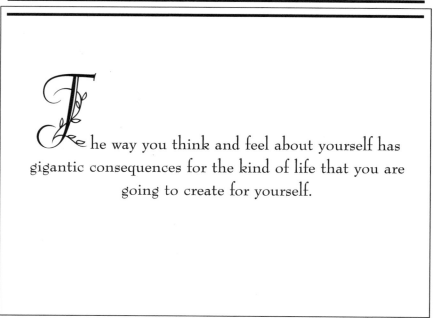

The way you think and feel about yourself has gigantic consequences for the kind of life that you are going to create for yourself.

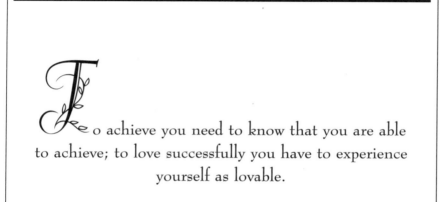

To achieve you need to know that you are able to achieve; to love successfully you have to experience yourself as lovable.

If you are convinced that happiness is your birthright and that happiness is the natural order of things, you will spontaneously tend to act in ways that will produce more happiness than unhappiness in your life.

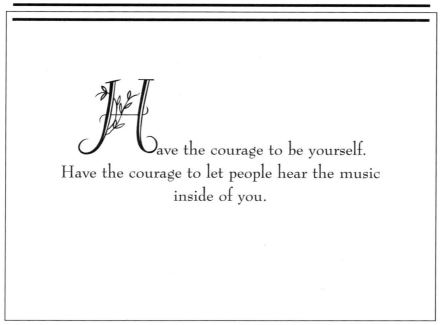

Have the courage to be yourself.
Have the courage to let people hear the music inside of you.

You build your self-esteem every time you are willing to stand up for who you are and express in appropriate ways what you think and what you feel.

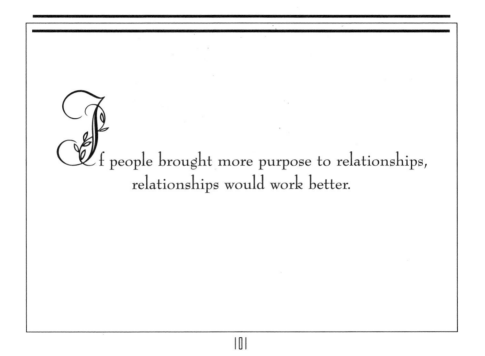

If people brought more purpose to relationships, relationships would work better.

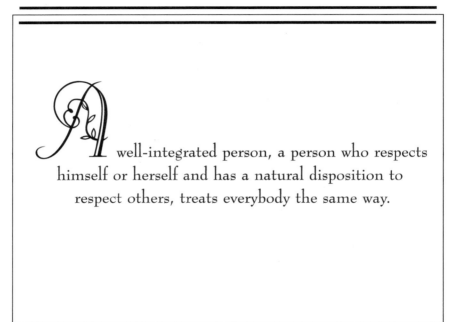

A well-integrated person, a person who respects himself or herself and has a natural disposition to respect others, treats everybody the same way.

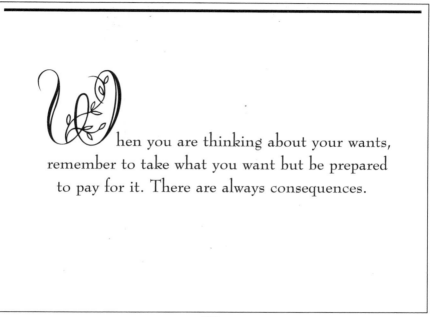

When you are thinking about your wants, remember to take what you want but be prepared to pay for it. There are always consequences.

Set goals that don't feel all that easy, that challenge you, that stimulate you, and that give you the chance to push yourself. That is where the power of growth lies.

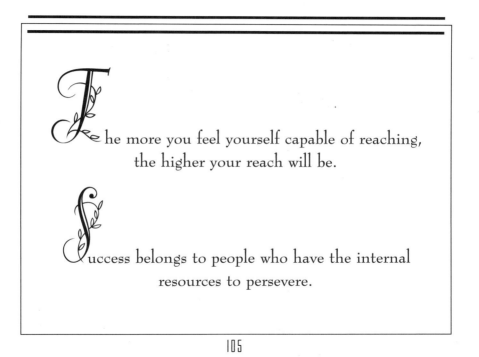

The more you feel yourself capable of reaching, the higher your reach will be.

Success belongs to people who have the internal resources to persevere.

Watch the tendency to blow up and catastrophize setbacks and treat them as if life has now said its last word on you and your possibilities, because that is not true unless you choose to make it true.

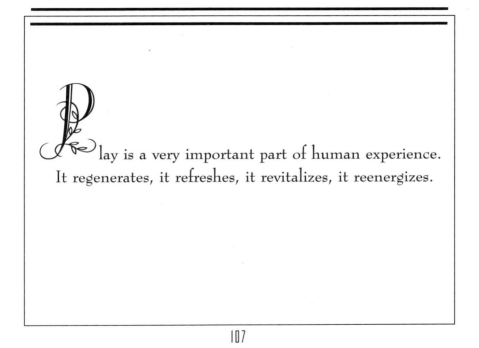

Play is a very important part of human experience. It regenerates, it refreshes, it revitalizes, it reenergizes.

You give your life structure and focus through your goals and purposes.

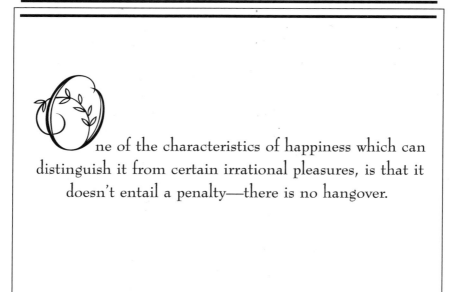

One of the characteristics of happiness which can distinguish it from certain irrational pleasures, is that it doesn't entail a penalty—there is no hangover.

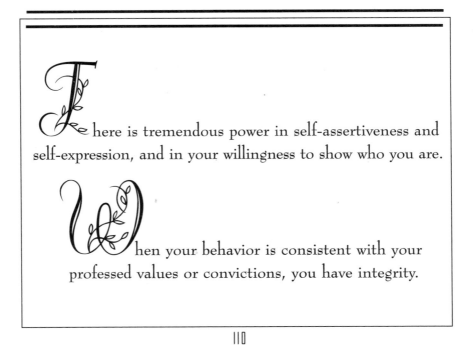

There is tremendous power in self-assertiveness and self-expression, and in your willingness to show who you are.

When your behavior is consistent with your professed values or convictions, you have integrity.

Yours is the most important opinion in the world. It is you you've got to impress. Self-esteem is the reputation you get with yourself.

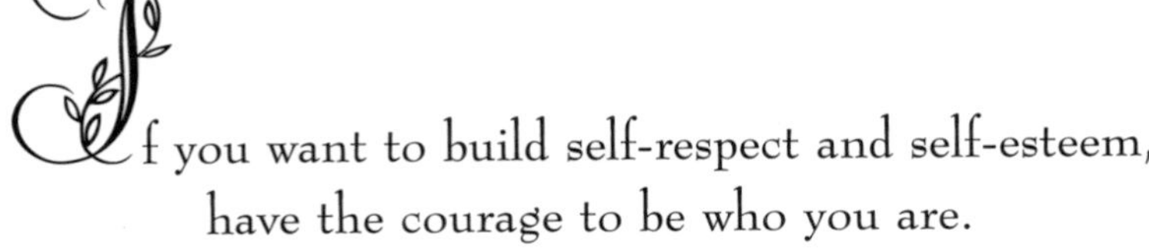

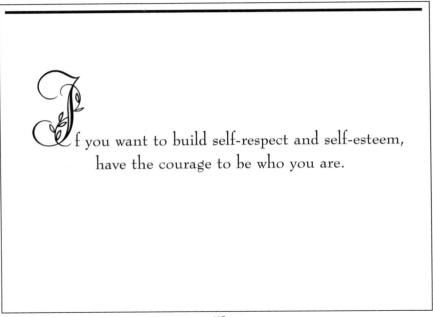

If you want to build self-respect and self-esteem, have the courage to be who you are.

If you feel confident in your own strength and abilities, and about your right to be happy, the natural impulse will be to set goals that challenge yourself and give you a chance to exercise your faculties.

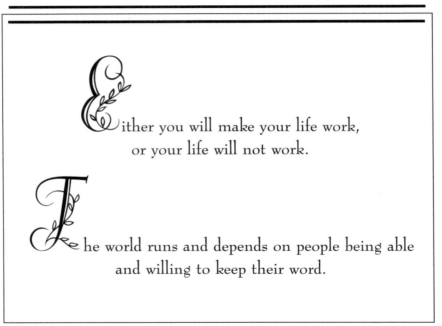

Either you will make your life work,
or your life will not work.

The world runs and depends on people being able
and willing to keep their word.

If you can give the kind of acknowledgment or feedback that allows people to feel that they have really been paid attention to, then you are a good listener.

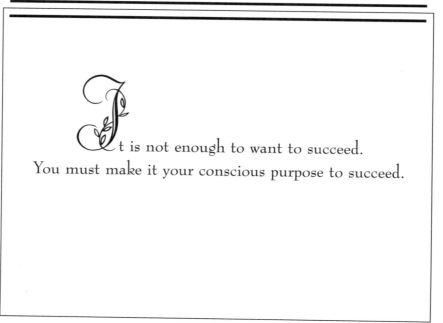

It is not enough to want to succeed. You must make it your conscious purpose to succeed.

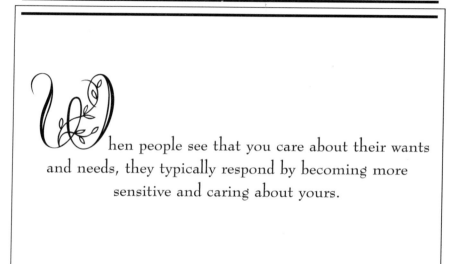

When people see that you care about their wants and needs, they typically respond by becoming more sensitive and caring about yours.

In the end, the one and only thing on which you can rely is your own mind, your own consciousness, and your own dedication to using it.

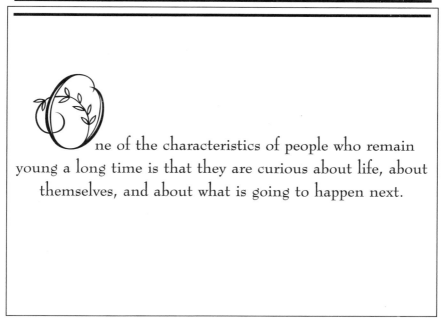

One of the characteristics of people who remain young a long time is that they are curious about life, about themselves, and about what is going to happen next.

The spirit of embracing life means embracing the challenges of life and not whining about them.

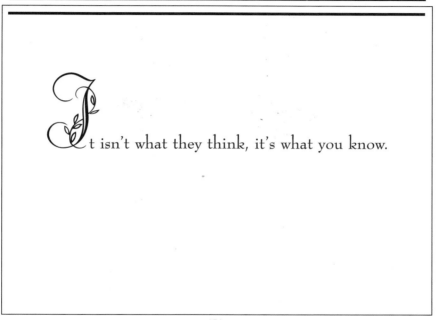

It isn't what they think, it's what you know.